not a guide to
Bridlington

Patricia Susan
Dixon MacArthur

The
History
Press

First published 2013

The History Press
The Mill, Brimscombe Port
Stroud, Gloucestershire, GL5 2QG
www.thehistorypress.co.uk

British Library Cataloguing in Publication Data.
A catalogue record for this book is available from the British Library.

ISBN 978 0 7524 9920 8

Typesetting and origination by The History Press
Printed in Great Britain

The Arms of Bridlington

The small crown or coronet at the top is composed of eight roses set upon a rim, from which a red sun is rising.

*

The shield comprises three capital letters, each a 'B' counterchanged in black and white. This is thought to be a repetition of the initial 'B' of Bridlington. Its threefold nature most likely denotes the doctrine of the Holy Trinity.

*

A broad band across the upper third of the shield has an indented edge resembling battlements and two little blue wavy bars.

*

The armorial belonged to the priory and was anciently one of the priory seals. The arms of the priory were assumed as the arms of the town.

*

The motto comprises: *signum* (symbol of); *salutis* (health, prosperity, safety or wellbeing); *semper* (always).

Contents

Bridlington

The town's original name, Bretlington, is listed in the Domesday Book of 1086.

Variations recorded in documents include: Brilinton (1135); Brillingtona (1138); Brellintun (1143); Bridlington (1201); Berlington and Breddelinton (1203); Brellington; Bolington (in a patent granted in 1315); Burling (1652).

The origins of the town's name are uncertain, but it is most probably named after a man – perhaps the Anglo-Saxon chieftain 'Bretel' or 'Beohrtel' (hence 'Bretel's tun', 'Bretelan tun' or 'Beohrtel's Farm'; a 'tun' is an enclosed homestead).

Alternatively, the Bridlings could be descendants of Bridla, a Saxon chieftain who established a settlement here.

The least popular theory is that the name derives from the Norse word *berlingr*, meaning 'smooth water' (i.e. Bridlington Bay).

Street Names

Bridlington's street names reflect its history, its link to the sea and the utilitarian logic of the locals.

Historical links to the Augustinian priory include Applegarth Lane (the canon's orchard); St John Street; Baylegate; and Woldgate (street/lane to the wold), the Roman route to York. The High Street was the Roman route to Malton.

Sea-linked names include Admirals Mews, Nelson Street, Neptune Street, and North Marine Drive.

Utilitarian names include Brick Kiln Balk (Bessingby), a lane to the brick kiln; Flag Lane, which led to a stonemason's; Fort Terrace and Garrison Street, which once had a fort/garrison at the end of the road; Fortyfoot, a 40ft-wide thoroughfare; Lime Kiln Lane, which led to the lime kiln; Long Lane (which, as it sounds, is a long lane!); Market Street, the site of the market; Pinfold Lane, which led to a pin fold (a circular enclosure for animals); Mill Lane, which once had a windmill where individuals brought their corn to be ground. The avenues were numbered, one to eight, rather than named – rather unimaginative!

Many Bridlington streets are named after people. Examples include: Amy Johnson Avenue, in honour of the famous aviatrix; Brett Street, named after one Dr Brett; Bronte Walk, after the writers; the Crayke, previously owned by the Crayke family; Prickett Road, after the Revd Dr Marmaduke Prickett; Squire Lane, after Mr Collinson, an original Feoffee, who left a wain way (cart way) through Collinson Garth. This survives as Squire Lane.

Auburn Close and Owthorne Close were named after the lost villages of Auburn and Owthorne (which stood near to Withernsea) before they were washed into the sea.

Some Quirky Names
Butts Close, Dragon Lane, Gypsey Bank, The Glimpse, Savage Road, Sheeprake Lane, Spion Kop.

Areas and Wards of Bridlington

Bridlington is in the East Riding of Yorkshire, and is the place where the countryside of the Yorkshire Wolds meets the sea.

Areas

Bridlington developed as two separate settlements: Burlington and Bridlington Quay. The medieval Old Town of Burlington, a market town 1 mile inland, was built around the Augustinian monastery. The Quay, meanwhile, was developed at the mouth of the Gypsey Race (now Clough Hole), in the harbour. The two settlements had already joined together by the time the railway arrived in 1846.

Bridlington Town Council Wards (since 2000):

Bridlington North

Bridlington Central and Old Town

Bridlington South

Bridlington North has an award-winning sand and shingle beach, and an Edwardian-themed promenade with views of the Heritage Coast (including the impressive Flamborough Cliffs).

Bridlington South has an award-winning sandy beach and nautical-themed promenade with wooden decking and beach huts.

Distance from...

	Miles	Kilometres
Ayers Rock, Australia	9,261	14,905
Brussels, Belgium	296	476
Centre of the Earth	3,959	6,371
Death Valley, USA	5,162	8,312
Eiffel Tower, Paris	376	605
Frankfurt, Germany	467	752
Guernsey, Channel Isles	337	543
Hong Kong, China	5,901	9,497
Isle of Man	175	281
Jerusalem, Israel	2,319	3,734
The Kremlin, Russia	1,492	2,401
London Eye	179	289
The Moon (average distance)	236,716	380,957
The North Pole	4,056	6,527
Osaka, Japan	5,774	9,293
The Panama Canal, Panama	5,283	8,501
Queenstown, New Zealand	11,634	18,723
Reykjavik, Iceland	1,031	1,660
The Sun (average distance)	92,850,000	149,427,590
The Taj Mahal, India	4,262	6,859
Ural Mountains, Russia	2,225	3,581
Vatican City, Italy	1,024	1,647
Washington DC	3,618	5,822
Xanthi, Greece	1,461	2,352
Yellowstone Park, Wyoming	4,482	7,212
Zurich, Switzerland	602	969

Twinned Towns

Bad Salzuflen, Germany

A favourite feel-good spa town in the Lippe district of
North Rhine-Westphalia, at the foot of the Teutoburg Forest,
and known for its nine sparkling salt-water springs (with
healing energies), and its thermal baths. Many historical
buildings may be found here, and houses preserved from
the sixteenth and seventeenth century. Formerly the town
profited from the salt trade, but it is now committed to health,
fitness and outdoor pursuits. It has a Nordic walking park, set
amidst rolling hills. The town's population is approximately
55,020 inhabitants, and twinning took place in 1976.

Millau, France (pronounced with no L sound, as *mee oh*)

A town in Southern France located at the confluence of the
Tarn and Dourbie rivers. There was a settlement on the spot
by the first century AD. A major Roman site and earthenware
centre, 'Contagomagus' supplied quality pottery right across
the Roman Empire for 150 years. Peace activists have lived
in a commune here since the 1970s. The town is known for
its gloves and, most recently, for the elegant Millau viaduct,
the tallest cable-stayed road bridge in the world. It has a
population of around 23,000, and twinning took place in
Bridlington on 12 April 1992, in a packed Leisure World.
Over 160 citizens from Millau – and their host families –
witnessed the signing of the twinning agreement.

Other Bridlingtons

There are no other Bridlingtons in the world. However, there are a few familiar names to be found:

Brislington, a parish in Bristol

Burlington, a city in Ontario, Canada. This is possibly named after Bridlington

Burlington, an incorporated town in Newfoundland, Canada

Burlington, a populated place in Victoria, Australia

Burlington, an unincorporated area on Prince Edward Island

Burlington Borough, Pennsylvania, USA

Burlington township in Burlington County, New Jersey, USA

Burlington township, Minnesota, USA

In the USA there is a Burlington City in Colorado, Iowa, Kansas, North Carolina, North Dakota, Vermont, Washington, and Wisconsin.

Also in the USA are seven Burlington towns, in Connecticut, Indiana, Maine, Massachusetts, New York, Otsego County, and Wisconsin.

Other Burlingtons include:

Burlington County, New Jersey, USA

Burlington Junction, a city in Missouri, USA

Historical Timeline

Roman road placed across the Wolds straight from York to Bridlington. Settlement at mouth of Gypsey Race (Castleburn).

Arrowheads left in man-made earthworks at Danes Dyke.

Retreat of Ice Age. First settlers arrive.

'Bretlington', the head of the Huntou Hundreds, is mentioned in the Domesday Book as well as the church. The port existed, but is not recorded.

Dissolution of the monastery at Bridlington, and execution of the last prior, William Wode. The manor of Bridlington and other possessions seized by the Crown.

St John of Bridlington canonised.

8000 BC	c. 2000 BC	c. 200	1086		1401	1537
c. 1600 BC	600 BC	1072	1113	1388		1630

Stone Age. Tallest monolith (7.6m) in the UK brought to Rudston.

Bay of the Gabrantvices; territory of the Parisi tribe.

Manor of Bridlington, confiscated from Earl Morcar by William the Conqueror, given to his nephew, Gilbert de Gant (c. 1040-1095).

Walter de Gant (c. 1087-1139) founded the Augustinian Monastery.

Bayle erected.

Manor of Bridlington purchased from Sir George Ramsey by thirteen inhabitants of the town. The Great Town Deed was drawn up, empowering the men as Lords Feoffees.

Discovery of a chalybeate spring (water with health-giving properties).

Corn Exchange built in Market Place, and the first RNLI lifeboat started service.

Aircraftsman Shaw (better known as Lawrence of Arabia) stationed in Bridlington. No. 1104 Marine Craft unit formed and based in the harbour.

Town's first bank (Burlington), hotel (The George, 1805) and lifeboat (1805) opened / launched.

Seafront lit by electricity.

900th anniversary of the founding of Bridlington Priory.

The arrival of the railway.

Dominican convent opened.

c. 1738   1802   1824 1846   1894   1930   1933   2013

1779   1811   1833   1881   1896   1931   1976

John Wesley preached in Zion Congregational church.

Gas service introduced to the town, and Temperance Hall built.

Donkey rides introduced on beach.

Severe gribble (a type of worm) infestation at the harbour.

Tidal spring discovered. The quay developed in the nineteenth century to become a seaside resort.

Courthouse and police station built.

Fish wharf and market built on South Pier; North Sea Wall finished.

Freak Weather

Severe gales were recorded in Bridlington in 1537, 1562, 1581, 1591, 1643, 1697 and 1717.

1554: A storm destroyed 110ft of the North Pier: the remainder was 'sore shaken and bruised by the same storm' and was in danger of 'suck from the sea' [*sic*].

1871: The Great Gale. Many lives were lost at sea.

1894: Much property destroyed in the Great Storm.

1901: Another 'great gale'. Three drowned.

1953: East Coast North Sea Floods affected England, Scotland, Belgium and the Netherlands. Hundreds of people died.

October 2010: Winds and high tides. 60ft waves crash onto the seafront, causing damage to rides and the seafront itself.

October 2010-Jan 2011: Snow havoc. Trains disrupted.

March 2011: Hottest place in the country for two days, with a temperature of 17 degrees Celsius.

October 2011: Hottest October day ever (3rd), with 25 degrees Celsius recorded at 3.15 p.m. Bridlington's previous record was 22.1 degrees Celsius (October 1978).

November 2011: Driest place in the United Kingdom, with only 11mm of rain, against a national average of 49mm (Meteogroup). High winds of 95mph hit Bridlington.

January 2012: 95mph high winds prevent Bridlington fishing fleet from going to sea, cause widespread disruption to trains on the East Coast mainline, uproot trees on Thornton Road and Eighth Avenue and tear down the Cricketers Arms' sign and an advertising sign on Quay Road. Boarding from building work on the Promenade was blown into the road. The Humber and Ouse bridges were closed, and householders were asked to bring in their bins to avoid them being blown over and causing further disruption.

A Day in the Life of the Town

03:00 Late-night revellers return home from pubs and clubs.

04:00 Seals occupy the beach before the dog walkers.

05:00 Seagulls squawk and patrol the pavements scavenging bins.

06:00 Strawberry field's car-boot sale/market sets up till 3 p.m. Bridlington Surf forecast issued.

07:00 Bridlington Park and Ride opens.

08:30 Tandem or accelerated skydives occurring. Prior John's Wetherspoons pub opens. Bridlington Bay boat launch opens.

09:00 Pensioners or 'ebayer's' queue at the Post Office. First bus of schoolchildren arrive at Leisure World Swimming Pool. Bridlington Lifeboat Station opens to the public.

11:00 Bayle Museum opens.

12:30 Schoolchildren swarm food outlets.

13:00 Bridlington Town Council office closes.

13:30 Gala bingo players settle to the main event of the afternoon.

14:00 Practice balls being hurled on Westgate Bowling Green.

15:00 Seafronts, amusement arcades, beaches and harbour, all thronging with people in summer – and deserted in winter.

19:00 Spa and Spotlight Theatre Shows. Diners order their meals.

21:00 Nightclubs begin livening up.

How Many Times a Year?

1

Once a year, approximately 1,500 scooters attend the Bridlington Scooter Rally. Around 3,500 people come along too.

9

The number of people bitten by donkeys in the summer of 1976 on Bridlington beaches.

52

The number of times a year that the *Bridlington Free Press*, the local newspaper, is published. Founded in 1859, it celebrated its 150th anniversary in 2009.

60

The number of times the lifeboat was called out in 2008.

451

The number of people bitten by insects on Bridlington beaches during the summer of 1976.

572

Priory church holds 572 regular services each year, plus many additional annual services for Christmas, Easter and St George's Day – as well as baptisms, marriages and funerals.

1,406

The number of times the tide comes in and goes out in 2013.

168,000

The number of times a new visitor entered Bridlington's Tourist Information Office in 2011.

25

Demographics

Figures from Bridlington's 2011 Census:
Total number of people: 35,369

Males: 17,037

Females: 18,332

Single people: 8,037

Married: 14,433

Divorced or widowed: 6,452

Ethnicity
White British: 34,278

Largest minority ethnic group: Indian (71)

Religion
Christian: 23,420

No religion: 9,043

Not stating a religion: 2,615

Buddhist: 70

Muslim: 51

Hindu: 27

Jewish: 18

Sikh: 16

Other: 109

Strange Statistics, Facts and Figures

£3.70-£7: Rental cost, per week, for a beach chalet in 1978.

25 per cent: Percentage of England's total lobster catch landed at Bridlington's Port, making it the largest lobster landing port in England (as of December 2011).

43 per cent: The number of visitors to Bridlington who stayed in overnight accommodation in 2011.

£45-£105: Cost per week for a beach chalet in 2012.

90mph: The speed at which Lawrence of Arabia once rode a motorcycle along the Promenade.

360: The number of vehicles which received parking tickets in Bridlington during the East Riding of Yorkshire Council's first month in charge of parking in the town, in 2011.

379: The number of taxpayers who paid a Poll Tax in Bridlington in 1377.

675: Number of seats in the Spa Theatre.

3,741: Town's population – living in 869 houses – in 1811.

3,800: Maximum standing capacity of the Spa Royal Hall.

£4,200: The price paid by thirteen prominent townsmen for the manor of Bridlington in 1630.

£45,000: Price paid for Sewerby Estate in 1934.

66,000: The number of visitors to Bempton Cliffs RSPB Reserve in 2009.

92,000 tonnes: Amount per annum of indirectly-fired kilned malt produced by Muntons Malt, Bridlington, in 2012.

£127,014: Average house price in Bridlington in 2012.

£1.4 million: Price spent on the government-funded travellers' site in Bridlington's Woldgate in 2012. It has twenty-two pitches, and includes a warden's block and a five-space car park.

Literary Quotations

'The vast green view of Bridlington North beach
shimmering … she threw her bottom on the sandy
beach and let the sea breathe in and out on her.'

From 'The Seashells of Bridlington North Beach'
(written for Mercy Angela), the marvellous poem
by Jack Mapanje (born in 1944 in Malawi)

'Although he had been born and bred in the town, Wilf
had never been inside the Priory Church … the men had
trouble placing their rifles as they entered … It was only
a short march to the Old Town Market Place where the
men were dismissed.'

***Life's Golden Time* (1985), Bette Vickers**

'…she did find it hard to stomach when a gilt-edged
invitation arrived asking them all to go to the unveiling
of the cenotaph which held every name of the
Bridlington lads who had been killed.'

***Ha'Penny Top and Farthing Tail* (1986), Bette Vickers**

'And then came the great invasion – of evacuees …
we got three … On the visit, the parents looked worse
than the kids … When the pubs closed the visitors
flooded the street, singing, shouting and arguing, most
of them the worse for drink.'

***Time to Pick the Flowers* (1989), Bette Vickers**

'…the neighbours sniffed as neighbours do … Bugger Brid!'

Jake Thackeray's song 'The Hair of the Widow
of Bridlington', which mocked Bridlington for
the small-mindedness of its inhabitants

Five books by Bette Vickers set, or partially set, in
Bridlington:

*Fed Up to Top Attic, Life's Golden Time, Ha'Penny Top and
Farthing Tail, Time to Pick the Flowers, The Ragged Arsed
Militia Boy.*

What the Famous Have Said About Bridlington

'No one dreams about going to Brid.'

A remark by Jeremy Clarkson which caused much annoyance in the town

'Sometimes we used to set off early so we could go to the seaside before [a gig in Hull]. I think Bridlington is the nearest place, so we'd go there.'

Jarvis Cocker

'Bridlington is the perfect place for me to come.'

Norman Cook, aka Fatboy Slim. On his Five Night Stand tour, visiting 'spiritual Meccas' of dance music

'Bridlington is on the road to nowhere. Only those who want to come to the town would make a visit.'

David Hockney. Hockney often speaks of his love of the local scenery, and the quiet nature of Bridlington.

'I'd never heard of Bridlington Spa before but I thought "that's a cool name." I'm loving it here.'

Jessie J at her 2011 concert

'Summer holidays in Scarborough or Bridlington were taken up with games of cricket on the beach.'

Sir Michael Parkinson CBE

'Bridlington in winter is a silent place, where cats and landladies' husbands walk gently down the middle of the streets. I prefer it to the hustle of summer.'

Lawrence of Arabia, known in the town as Aircraftsman T.E. Shaw

'The greatest absurdity.'

Charlotte Bronte referring to the local's habit of promenading

Famous For...

Fish and chips, bucket-and-spade seaside holidays and **North Sea fishing**.

Surfing: Bridlington is the first recorded place in Britain where surfing took place, during the 1890 visit of two Hawaiian princes, Prince Jonah Kūhiō Kalaniana'ole Pi'ikoi and his brother Prince David Kahalepouli Pi'ikoi.

The 100-year-old Bridlington-built sailing coble *Three Brothers* (built in 1912).

William of Newburgh or Newbury (*c.* 1136-*c.* 1198), also known as William Parvus, a twelfth-century historian and Augustinian canon from Bridlington. His *Historia rerum Anglicarum*, a history of England from 1066 to 1198, is valued for detailing the Anarchy under Stephen of England. This book, intriguingly, is also a major source for stories of medieval revenants – i.e. those souls thought by medieval readers to return from the dead, including early vampire stories. It is also the only source for the bishop-pirate Wimund.

Peter Langtoft (*c.* 1305), historian and chronicler. Peter was an Augustinian monk at Bridlington Priory, and wrote a history of England, from the founding of Britain by Brutus to the death of King Edward I, in Anglo-Norman verse. It is popularly known as *Langtoft's Chronicle*. Nine 'songs' capture soldier's taunts during the Anglo-Scottish conflicts of the late thirteenth and early fourteenth centuries.

St John of Bridlington (*c.* 1320-1379), formerly John of Thwing, the last Englishman to be made a saint before the Reformation. Credited with many miracles, including walking on the sea to rescue sailors caught in a storm, turning water to wine, raising the dead, multiplying corn, curing the sick and foretelling the hour of his own death. Patron saint of women in difficult labour, and of fishermen.

George Ripley (*c.* 1415-1490), an important English alchemist. Canon at Bridlington in the latter fifteenth century. Journeyed through France, Germany and Italy, and lived in Rome. He wrote the *Compound of Alchemy* and many works in verse. Died in Bridlington, and was buried in the priory.

William Kent (*c.* 1685-1748), baptised (in 1686) as William Cant. Bridlington-born, he was a nationally renowned painter, eminent architect, landscape architect and furniture designer. He was born at 74 High Street.

Samuel Standidge (1725-1801), Bridlington-born sea captain and father of the whaling industry in Hull. Knighted by George II.

John Matson (1760-1826), who built Flamborough Lighthouse (85ft tall, standing on a chalk cliff 170ft high) in 1806 without the use of scaffolding.

Benjamin Fawcett (1808-1893), Bridlington-born Woodblock colour-printing pioneer. His masterpiece is the hand-coloured wood engravings he produced for Francis Orpen Morris's *British Birds*, which had a profound effect on British ornithology.

Humphrey Sandwith (1822-1881), Bridlington-born doctor of the Crimean era. He was inspector general of hospitals.

John Taylor Allerston (1828-1914), a Bridlington-born artist and son of an Old Town draper. Specialised in coastal scenes, and maritime scenes in oil and watercolour. Paintings of Bridlington include one of the Great Gale of 1871.

'May' Kendall (1861-1931). Born Emma Goldsworth Kendall, this Bridlington-born Victorian poet, novelist, satirist and reformer worked with the Rowntree family of York. Her poem *Lay of the Trilobite* condemns the 'advance' of civilisation.

Edmund Johnston Garwood (1864-1949), Bridlington-born British geologist.

Alfred Edward 'A.E.' Matthews OBE (1869-1960), Bridlington-born stage and film actor for eight decades. His birthplace, on the site of the current B&Q store, is today recognised with a blue plaque. Aged eighty-nine he sat, for several days and nights, on the pavement outside his London home to prevent the council installing a streetlight. Spike Milligan penned an episode of the Goon Show entitled *The Evils of Bushey Spon* based on the incident.

Cricketer David Cecil Fowler Burton (1887-1971), known as Cecil Burton, captained Yorkshire from 1919 to 1921. His younger brother (Robert) Claude Burton (1891-1971) made two appearances for Yorkshire in the 1914 season.

Wallace Hartley (1878-1912), who got his band together to play as the *Titanic* sank. He led a quintet. As there was also a trio on board, all seven musicians played together for the first – and last – time as the ship went down. Before his appointment aboard the ship, Hartley had moved to Bridlington (in his twenties) to join the local Municipal Orchestra.

Winifred Holtby (1898-1935), a Rudston-born novelist and journalist who is best known for her novel *South Riding*, about a fictitious Yorkshire community – which resembles Bridlington – struggling with the Depression of the 1930s.

Herbert Leslie Gee (1901-1977), a Bridlington-born writer (pen name Francis Gay). Wrote for the *Methodist Recorder* as the 'friendly man', and was the man behind *The Friendship Book*.

Amy Johnson (1903-1941). The grandparents of the famous aviatrix lived here, and her parents retired here. She spent a lot of her childhood holidays in Bridlington.

Walter Goodin (1907-1992), an artist who lived in the town. Painted panoramic images of the Wolds, East Yorkshire coastline and Bridlington.

Francis Frederick Johnson CBE (1911-1995), Bridlington-born architect, designed a number of churches (including Sewerby Methodist Church, 1963).

Paul Hardwick (1918-1983), Bridlington-born actor known for films such as *The Prince and the Showgirl* with Marilyn Monroe.

Helene Palmer (1928-2011), British actress known for her portrayal of *Coronation Street*'s Ida Clough. Originally from the West Riding, she moved to Bridlington in 1986; she ran and lived at Nag's Head pub in Market Place until 1990, when she moved to Sewerby.

Robert 'Bob' Wallis (1934-1991), Bridlington-born Jazz musician. Successful in the early 1960s, and played predominantly with the Storyville Jazzmen.

Michael John 'Mick' Pyne (1940-1995), Bridlington-raised jazz musician (piano, trumpet, saxophone, arrangements) and his brother **Norman Christopher 'Chris' Pyne** (1939-1995), a Bridlington-born jazz trombonist.

Infamous for...

Lazy winds, a bitterly cold easterly wind that goes through you rather than around.

Areas of Bridlington surrounding the harbour: these had the highest percentage of homes in fuel poverty in the East Riding in December 2011.

Over fifty dummy parking tickets were issued to law-breaking motorists by East Riding of Yorkshire Council enforcement officers during the two weeks (until 7 November 2011) when they took over from Humberside Police traffic wardens.

The loss of the shipping industry. Twenty trawlers operated out of Bridlington fifteen years ago. None operated in 2012.

Greedy, vicious seagulls: these will swoop and take the food you're eating. Have been known to scratch people's heads whilst protecting their young.

Lots of traffic lights and traffic-calming humps. The St John's Avenue humps were originally too high and had to be reduced.

Making the Headlines

The Harbour East Riding Yorkshire Council threatened to use compulsory powers to acquire and develop land on Bridlington Harbour as part of their Area Action Regeneration Plan. Harbour Commissioners vowed to fight against it. During 2012 a new £260,000 tidal mini-marina created pontoon berths for another sixty-six boats (from 20ft cabin cruisers to 40ft ocean-going yachts) inside the current harbour – all utilising commissioner's funds.

Bridlington Hospital (opened in 1989) regularly makes the headlines for its lack of services: no A&E, maternity wing or cardiology; empty wards; people forced to travel in the early hours of the morning to and from Scarborough Hospital. More positively for the refurbishment project, the new menus for the canteen are created by celebrity chef James Martin; also, the merger of York Teaching Hospital NHS Foundation Trust and Scarborough and North East Yorkshire NHS Trust began in July 2012.

Each time that new plans for wind turbines are submitted they are fought off. David Hockney was against them for spoiling the Wolds' landscape. MP Greg Knight supported the Wolds' anti-wind farm protesters. Even the MOD joined the protest, claiming a detrimental effect on the operation of the Air Defence Radar at Staxton Wold in 2011.

Bridlington is one of the worst areas for metal theft. The soaring price of metal worldwide led to twenty-two reported cable thefts from Scarborough, Bridlington and Hull railway lines between March 2011 and November 2011. Also targeted were utilities substations and businesses including churches, schools and hospital roofs. Police had to crack down, stopping and searching vehicles and visiting scrap yards.

In March 2011 reports revealed that there were fifty-one empty and boarded-up shops' premises in the town, with not enough quality stores and too many charity shops and shops selling cheap goods. By 2012, an influx of pawnbroking and moneylending chains was noted.

45

Letters to the Press

The letters page of the *Bridlington Free Press* has hosted many debates on the topics of the harbour (whether or not to create a marina or a mini-marina), hospital services (or the lack of them), and shops and shopping in the town.

Regarding wind turbines, the letters are mostly set against, claiming that they are an eyesore, tend to be ineffective, and that the flickering effect from the sun's light bouncing off the blades will distract drivers; it has also been suggested that they emit a constant low-frequency noise and kill bats and birds. Supporters refute all claims.

David Hockney is frequently mentioned and applauded for his art, his utterances and all he has done for the area.

The almost daily problem of fly-tipping on Woldgate crops up often.

The condition of the sea water and beaches – either in praise or in condemnation – frequently prompts a letter to the press, as does the problem of homelessness, bin collections (frequency) and public toilets (their closure, location and condition).

Dog dirt on the streets clearly concerns a great many residents. Also the noise, mess and harm to humans caused by seagulls (including the issue of whether or not to cull them).

Car-parking debates concentrate on the lack of it, the need for more, the desire for free town parking and opposition to (or support for) the Lords Feoffees' plan for a multi-storey car park. Associated issues include East Riding Yorkshire Council's treatment of Blue Badge holders and the high frequency of parking fines (leading some people to wonder if wardens are under pressure to get tickets...).

Road conditions often prompt a letter on potholes and lack of gritting.

Bridlington has many mobility scooters, leading to letters about the safety of pedestrians on the pavements with riders speeding or causing accidents, and calls for scooters to be insured like cars.

Rebellious Bridlington

1536: The last Bridlington prior, William Wood, was executed at Tyburn for his part in the Catholic rebellion known as the Pilgrimage of Grace, a protest against Henry VIII's break with the Roman Catholic Church and the Dissolution of the Monasteries.

c. **1844:** Locals resisted the developer's desire to build the railway station at Bridlington Quay, near the harbour and beaches. A petition by the inhabitants of Old Town resulted in it being located midway between the two settlements.

1900: Strike of Bridlington joiners, who demanded a pay rise from 7*s* 5*d* to 8*s* 5*d*.

1974: East Yorkshire Action Group formed after East Riding County Council was abolished and the County of Humberside created. Campaign against Humberside successful in 1995.

2008: 7,000 people turned out for a mass rally protesting at proposed cuts to the services at Bridlington Hospital.

2012: Pensioners' Action Group East Riding (PAGER) are active campaigners. In May 2012, MP Greg Knight received the pensioners' transport petition concerning concessionary travel for pensioners.

Buildings and Architecture

Oldest and Tallest
Priory church, founded by Walter de Gant in 1113. All that is left of the original church is the nave, which is now the parish church of St Mary the Virgin, a stunning example of medieval architecture. The imposing towers, designed by Sir Gilbert Scott, were not completed until 1875. The south-west tower is 150ft high.

Smallest

The first Baptist chapel in Bridlington. On Applegarth Lane, hidden behind a wall and iron railings, it was built in 1699 by Robert Prudom (*c.* 1655-1708), merchant, Lord Feoffee and founder of the Baptist church in Bridlington. A replica gravestone stands in the grounds. He lived in Baylegate.

Most controversial, ugliest and biggest eyesore
Ebor Flats. Built in the early 1970s, and completed in 1976, these are nine storeys (and 82ft) high. Ebor House, a development of thirty-five two-bedroom flats overlooking the harbour, was recently redesignated for applicants over forty years old.

The most rebuilt (and therefore the most expensive)

The Spa (Royal Hall) and Theatre. Bridlington Spa and Theatre is situated on the South Promenade on the seafront, adjacent to the harbour. The 'New Spa and Gardens' were built, together with the adjoining sea wall, in 1896, by Whitaker Brothers of Leeds. The lake was kept full by the iron-rich water of a Chalybeate spring. The theatre burnt down in October 1906, but was renovated and reopened in 1907 as the New Spa Opera House (designed by W.S. Walker).

The complex was bought by the corporation in 1919 for £16,000. The first 'Spa Royal Hall' was built at a cost of £50,000. Building work began in January 1926, and it opened that July. In 1932, however, Spa Royal Hall was destroyed by fire and totally rebuilt in five months. After the rebuilding, there were two cafés, a palm court, a solarium and a dance hall. The Spa closed in 2005 for extensive refurbishment, costing around £20 million, reopening in 2008.

November 2012 was the Spa Royal Hall's eightieth anniversary. The Royal Hall is still a magnificent 1930s Art-Deco ballroom. The Spa Theatre is an ornate, Edwardian two-tier theatre.

Most extraordinary

Royal Yorkshire Yacht Club, a substantial Victorian building on Windsor Crescent built in the late 1800s. It used to be the Ozone Hotel. Aircraftsman T.E. Shaw (better known as Lawrence of Arabia) lodged there. The hotel was renovated in the late 1930s in the style of a boat for the yacht club; the club took over in 1938.

Most desirable

The most desirable properties in Bridlington are those with a sea view – including North Marine Drive, South Marine Drive and Belvedere Parade. The two 'Norwegian' Houses are lovely south-side properties with excellent views. South Cliff and the Martongate area are also favoured.

Unusual Historic Building

The Bayle, the medieval gatehouse to Bridlington Priory, probably dates from soon after 1388, when a licence to fortify the priory was granted. Used in the Middle Ages for manorial courts, it once housed the town prison. Managed by the lords feoffees from 1630, the building is now a museum and the meeting place of the lords. It is today a Grade I listed building and Scheduled Ancient Monument.

Loveliest Public Building

Bridlington Town Hall was built in 1931 and opened in 1932. It was designed by F.Y. Newton (borough surveyor). Red brick, mostly two-storey and with double bronze doors, this civic building is located near to the centre of Bridlington, Station Avenue and Quay Road. Civil ceremonies can be booked. Grade II listed from 23 January 1989, the interior entrance hall has an imperial marble staircase, with panelled lobby beyond, leading to a panelled council chamber on the left and a ballroom to the right. Also contains the mayor's parlour.

Least Attractive Public Building

Crown Buildings.

Large hotels

The Expanse Hotel has forty-seven bedrooms (eight singles, two suites, three sea-facing club rooms/upgraded doubles, eighteen twin rooms, sixteen doubles) and five apartments.

The Monarch Hotel has forty-five bedrooms (four singles, three family and the rest double or twin).

The Balmoral Hotel has thirty-four bedrooms (three singles and the remainder are at least double rooms).

The Revelstoke Hotel is the next largest with twenty-eight rooms in total.

Developments

Promenades Shopping Centre opened in 1995. Phase two was completed in 2011, resulting in Bridlington's largest covered shopping centre at 75,000 sq. ft.

East Riding College, in the grounds of the former St George's School (previously Headlands Lower School); in the playing fields are two mounds, the remains of the archery butts used when men and boys had to practise archery every Sunday in case they were conscripted to fight. The new college building cost £17 million.

The Avenue, Westgate, was converted into dwellings in 1989. It was previously used as a hospital (maternity). The house was built in 1714 as a home for the Prickett family. The date can be seen on the original lead rainwater heads. The name comes from the avenue of trees leading from the park entrance to the front door.

Bridlington High School for Girls closed in 1977 after seventy-two years, to be merged with the grammar school as a comprehensive. The combined school finally closed in 2001, when it was partially demolished for a Barratt development.

Museums

The Bayle Museum
Once the gatehouse to Bridlington Priory, it has a history of over 800 years and will appeal to all ages. See a 1667 prison cell and a medieval lavatory.

Boyes Museum
Within the Boyes store, up on the top floor, is this period shop scene with displays and audio accompaniment. Admission is free.

Bridlington Harbour Heritage Museum
Celebrates Bridlington's rich maritime heritage.

Sewerby Hall
A fine example of an early Georgian house built between 1714-1720, with alterations made between 1808-1856, including a stable block, gatehouse and conservatory. Collection of memorabilia on display in tribute to Amy Johnson, donated in 1958 by her father. History of the Graeme family of Sewerby Hall and the local area.

Attractions

Amusement Arcades

Bempton Cliffs Seabirds

Bondville Miniature Village (Sewerby)

Burton Agnes Hall

Candy Kingdom

Danes Dyke

Fishing Trips

Flamborough Head and the Lighthouses

John Bull Rock Factory, Carnaby

Leisure World

Maritime Trail

Montyzoomers (children's indoor fun park)

North Marine Putting Green and Crazy Golf

Old Town Trail

Park Rose Carnaby and Animal Park & Bird of Prey Centre

Pitch & Putt Crazy Golf

Priory Church

RNLI Lifeboat House

Seafront Rides

Sewerby Hall, Zoo and Gardens

Speedboat Rides

Spotlight Theatre

The Spa

Woldgate Trekking Centre

Wold Top Brewery, Wold Newton

Yorkshire Belle Pleasure Steamer Cruises (Heritage Coast to Flamborough and Bempton birds)

Parks

Avenue Park, on Westgate, was opened in 1924 by Bridlington Corporation. It is now managed by East Riding of Yorkshire Council.

Dukes' Park, Queensgate, bequeathed in 1893. George Dukes left part of his estate to be a public park. It was taken over by Bridlington Corporation in 1921. Originally of 6 acres, it was doubled in size and the Queensgate football ground was laid out on adjoining land.

Gasworx Skate Park is run by Bridlington Town Council.

Queen's Park on Fortyfoot was opened in 1937 by Bridlington Corporation. It is now managed by East Riding of Yorkshire Council.

Sewerby Hall and gardens comprise of 50 acres of grounds, including landscaped gardens and woodland walks. It was in private ownership until 1934, when it was bought by Bridlington Corporation. Today it is owned by East Riding of Yorkshire Council.

Gardens

Bridlington has many small, managed gardens, including:

Beaconsfield Sunken Gardens, Northside

The Crescent Gardens

Fort Terrace

South Cliff Gardens

St Anne's Road secret garden

Lost Villages near Bridlington

The coastline near Bridlington was created from glacial till and it is constantly eroding. There are now twenty-eight lost villages and towns along the length of the Holderness coast, all of them taken by the encroaching sea. The till of East Yorkshire is considered to begin at Sewerby where the pre-glacial cliff turns inland.

Wilsthorpe was once a more extensive settlement, but by 1905 all the village had disappeared except one house, which was then 6ft from the cliff edge, but is now lost to the sea.

The village of Auburn was situated just below Wilsthorpe. Its decline may have begun with the plague, as its tax quota reduced by 55 per cent in 1534. The village comprised of seven houses and a chapel in 1716, but only three houses remained by 1731 when St Nicholas chapel was demolished. By 1815 the village had been abandoned to coastal erosion, except for a farm and a cottage; the 1841 census showed two households living at Auburn.

Hartburn was just south of Bridlington. By 1786 it had been entirely washed away.

A little further down the coast Hyde, Withow and Cleeton were also lost to the sea. Cleeton took its name from the nature of the soil, 'clay town'.

Abandoned Settlements

There are approximately 130 deserted villages in East Riding. Some were deserted in the Middle Ages, others de-populated in the eighteenth century. Economic decline, disasters like the plague, and clearance by landowners were the main causes.

The twelfth-century parish of Bridlington covered some 14,500 acres and included nine townships in addition to Bridlington itself – Bempton, Buckton, Easton, Grindale, Hilderthorpe, Marton, Sewerby, Speeton, Wilsthorpe and part of Auburn.

Along Kingsgate, and situated north of the golf course, earthworks mark the site of the former medieval village of Hilderthorpe.

Local Flora and Fauna

Seagulls are everywhere in Bridlington, mostly the large and noisy herring gull.

At Bempton there are more than 200,000 seabirds from April to August, including gannets, guillemots, razorbills, kittiwakes and fulmars – and, from April to July, puffins.

Sea life in the area includes crabs, lobsters, starfish, jellyfish, shellfish, fish, seals, dolphins, basking sharks and whales.

Sewerby Park Zoo has many animals, including llamas, peacocks, Humbolt penguins and Mandarin ducks.

Bridlington railway station's buffet and refreshment rooms always has an excellent and award-winning flower display.

Bridlington's Floral Clock was installed on the seafront, Prince's Parade, in 1907. It was relocated to Sewerby Hall and gardens in the late 1970s. Over 100 years old, the mechanism is in the Clock Tower tearooms.

Park Rose Birds of Prey & Animal Park, Carnaby, won the 'Start-up Business of the Year Award' in 2011 (Chamber Bridlington & Wolds' 2011 business awards).

Home-Grown Businesses

Forum Leisure Complex began as an amusement arcade in the 1930s and acquired the name 'Joyland' in 1936. In its heyday it was the largest privately owned amusement arcade and funfair in the UK. Today it is a large, family-owned entertainment complex with a multi-screen cinema, bar and carvery, ten-pin bowling, prize bingo and an extensive amusement arcade with all the latest games and videos.

Fish and Chips at 149 on Marton Road won the UK's 'chip shop of the year' award in January 2011.

Milner's Bakery has been trading for over fifty years on Quay Road. Family-owned, it is now run by the third generation. It supplies local cafés and restaurants, and caters for events and celebrations; new services added over the years include phone and post orders.

A. Brunton Waste Management, which offers skip hire and scrap-metal processing, has been in the recycling business for over 100 years; they've been located at their Boynton site since 1950.

Spotlight Theatre, home of Bridlington Amateur Operatic and Dramatic Society (BAODS, established in 1909), is a 120-seat theatre presenting a range of entertainment. It opened for its first performance in 2000.

Home-Grown Companies

Bridlington Shellfish Co. Ltd
Established in 2003 after the original company, Bridlington Trawlers, retired, this company now exports shellfish across the UK, and to France, Italy, Spain, Switzerland and Japan.

John Bull Confections Ltd
Representing over 100 years of rock-making by the same family, this business opened in 1911 in Prince Street. The Carnaby World of Rock site was developed in 1984. Now they have shops all over the UK.

Muntons Malt
Muntons has been producing malt, and malted ingredients, for over eighty years. They supply malts, malt extract, home-brew kits, flours and flakes. In the late 1950s malting facilities were expanded and moved closer to the Scottish whisky distillers. The site chosen was Bridlington, and the business opened in 1964. Developed and expanded during the 1990s, Muntons is one of the most modern and efficient maltings in Europe. Much of the barley is sourced locally, from the Yorkshire Wolds and from the Vale of York. They also produce distilling, brewing and food malts for both domestic and export markets.

West Building Supplies
For forty years an independent company, the company was begun by Chris West and Michael Heaton in October 1971. Supplying materials to the building trade and DIY market, as well as to the modular building and caravan industries, it employs forty staff on three sites.

Ernest Whiteley & Co.
The retirement of Ann Clough, the present owner, will see the end of an era. Her grandfather started the business in 1901, selling lingerie, fashions and drapery.

David Cooper Blacksmiths Ltd,
This ironworks forges using traditional blacksmithing techniques. A specialist in reproduction, restoration and conservation of period wrought iron, it also sells new and contemporary designs.

Political Figures

Andrew Hartley Dismore (Bridlington, 1954), British Labour Party politician, lawyer and MP for Hendon from 1997 until 2010. The son of an hotelier, he set the twenty-first-century record for a filibuster in the House of Commons by talking for 197 minutes.

Angela Eagle (Bridlington, 1961) is a British Labour Party politician; she has been MP for Wallasey since 1992. Daughter of a printworker, she was joined in the House of Commons at the 1997 general election by her twin sister, Maria Eagle – the first set of twins to sit in the House.

Maria Eagle (Bridlington, 1961) is a British solicitor and Labour Party politician. She is MP for Garston and Halewood, having been the MP for Liverpool Garston from 1997 to 2010. She is the shadow secretary of state for transport. Like her twin sister Angela, Maria Eagle is a very able chess player, having played for England, and a keen cricketer.

Thomas Davis Fenby (1875-1956). Born in Bridlington, a British Liberal politician and blacksmith, Fenby was the son of the master of a local blacksmith's forge. Elected Liberal MP for East Bradford in the 1924 general election, he often spoke in favour of smallholders in Parliament. He was made a Whip of the English Liberal MPs in 1926. Fenby espoused birth control and the abolition of capital punishment.

Greg Knight (1949), MP for Bridlington (Conservative), represents the East Yorkshire Constituency, which has included the town since 1997.

Sir John Major (1698-1781), 1st Baronet of Worlingsworth Hall. Born in Bridlington, he was a British merchant and MP for Scarborough in 1761.

Alderman John Sawden (1861-1910), mayor of Bridlington. Devoted twenty-five years to public service. His memorial drinking fountain was erected by public subscription.

Richard Frederick Wood (1920-2002), Baron of Holderness and MP for Bridlington, 1950-1979.

ERECTED
BY PUBLIC SUBSCRIPTION
TO THE MEMORY
OF
ALDERMAN
JOHN SAWDON
MAYOR OF DARLINGTON
1898-9 1902-3 1907-8
WHO DEVOTED 25 YEARS
TO PUBLIC SERVICE
IN THE BOROUGH AND ON
THE COUNTY COUNCIL

Scientific Discoveries

From 1876, the Plimsoll Line (the line or point on a ship's hull where it meets the water) had to be marked onto the outside of every ship, specifying the maximum load allowed aboard ship. This was a result of losses at sea, including those in the Great Gale of Bridlington Bay on 10 February 1871. Seventy lives were lost in less than twenty-four hours, including six lifeboatmen. Twenty-three known ships were wrecked but many others went down without a trace. Plimsoll believed the death toll would have been lower if the ships had not been so deeply laden and had been in better condition.

North Sea Marine Wildlife. Marine conservationists working off the North Sea Coast recorded 352 wildlife species. Of those, 126 were seaweeds, many previously unrecorded in the region.

Alchemy. Sir George Ripley (c. 1415-c. 1490), the canon of Bridlington, placed alchemy on a higher level than many of his contemporaries, considering it to be a spiritual rather than a physical affair. He maintained that alchemy is concerned with the mode of our spirit's return to the God who gave it to us. He wrote *The Compound of Alchemy; or, the Twelve Gates leading to the Discovery of the Philosopher's Stone*, dedicated to King Edward IV. His twenty-five-volume work brought him considerable fame. He also reportedly provided funds for the Knights of St John by means of the Philosopher's Stone he had concocted. Being particularly rich, he gave the general public some cause to believe in his ability to change base metal into gold.

Bridlington School headmaster Arthur Thornton, was, in 1896, the first to realise the future potential of X-rays for medical and industrial uses. He also understood that they might be employed to detect bombs or dangerous packages. After he came to Bridlington he was sometimes asked by local doctors to X-ray their patients, and some time later was asked to advise Lloyd Hospital on the setting up and use of X-ray equipment. Thornton Ward in the present hospital is named in his honour.

Local Characters, Past and Present

OYEZ, OYEZ, OYEZ… Town crier David Hinde was appointed by Bridlington Town Council in February 2012 – the first crier for 111 years. David claims to have one of the loudest cries in the country.

John Henry 'Goosey' Wilson (1858-1915): for years, the pet goose he couldn't eat for Christmas dinner followed him everywhere, at his heels, 'setting to' dogs and acting as a kind of guardian.

Christmas Day dippers: Over forty-five years of tradition lie behind this event, during which dozens of people, many in fancy dress, plunge into the sea at 10 a.m. on Christmas Day on North Beach to raise funds for local causes.

And an achievement of another kind: Thomas Newman died at the age of 153 years in 1542.

Crimes, Court Cases and Mysteries

At Skipsea, 7 miles south of Bridlington, Flemish adventurer Drogo de Bevere erected a fine motte-and-bailey castle. Having fought alongside William the Conqueror at the Battle of Hastings in 1066, he was honoured by being allowed to marry one of the king's nieces. He became Lord of Holderness and lived in the castle at Skipsea. One day he came to the king and asked to borrow some money so that he and his wife could visit Flanders. It was a lie: when suspicious staff searched the grounds after de Bevere had left, they found his wife's body. It was too late, however, to do anything about it: Drogo had fled, and was never seen again. Locals came to believe that he had poisoned his wife and buried her body because he thought she was a sorceress.

In 1284 Adam Newsom, lay brother at the priory, was imprisoned for killing Adam Grinton, the parish chaplain.

In 1396 the *Cristofre of Stanre* from Danzic (Gdańsk) was cast ashore by a tempest near 'Bridlyngton', and 'men of these parts seized her cargo'.

In 1705 the Revd Henock Sinclair, vicar of Owthorne, was killed by his servant Adam Alvin. After his death, Adam and the reverend's eldest niece, Mary, were married.

Smuggling was rife on the East Yorkshire coast, with many people from all sections of society involved. The forty-strong crew of the *Kent*, captained by notorious swashbuckler George 'Stoney' Fagg, was captured off Filey in July 1777, having been chased by two Revenue sloops, the *Prince of Wales* and the *Royal George*, and two naval frigates, the HMS *Pelican* and HMS *Arethusa*. HMS *Pelican* had chased the *Kent* out of Bridlington Bay the day before and lost her during the night.

Dr Edward William Pritchard (1825-1865), a Medical Officer in Bridlington, was hanged on 28 July 1865, on Glasgow Green, for poisoning his wife, mother-in-law and others. His was the last public execution in Scotland.

Ghosts and the Unexplained

The Revd Tom Willis (1930-) was born in Middlesborough, and settled in Bridlington in 1980. He has served the Church as an authorised Church of England Minister of Deliverance (the church's preferred term for an exorcist) in the York diocese for more than thirty years. Until his retirement, in 1996, he exercised his duties in the hidden ministry of the Church, casting out ghosts, poltergeists and evil spirits. He was also the Archbishop of York's special adviser on the occult. At that time the Archbishop was the Rt Revd David Hope.

Many properties in Bridlington High Street and Westgate have had rumours of ghostly encounters, including:

Ye Olde Star Inn, an old timbered building, parts of which were built in the 1600s, is allegedly haunted by a number of ghosts, including a little girl who died here and a man who sits on a stool at the end of the bar. There is a horse-mounting block in the yard.

More than one spirit wanders The Bayle, including a monk and an ex-prisoner once held in the Kidcote.

The footpath beside the graveyard at Priory church is said to be haunted.

At High Street Bookshop (Burlington Books), formerly a pharmacy, the owners have: been tapped on the shoulder by an invisible hand; heard phantom footsteps; seen the spirit of a little girl in a red coat run past; had crayons thrown at them; and seen gloopy drips drop from the ceiling, which then faded without leaving a trace.

One of the ghosts could be that of a lady who went for help at the pharmacy in 1916 after an Old Town encounter during which she was shot. Two young girls may also have died in a fire on the premises in the era before it became a pharmacy. It opened as a pharmacy in 1813; the interior was purpose-built, and the building still contains the original fittings. The cellars are lined with stone, probably taken from the priory.

The Bull and Sun is the most haunted pub in Bridlington, with many sightings of a Victorian ghost on the stairway. It is also the only public house in England of that name.

Burton Agnes Hall, near Bridlington, has an early seventeenth-century ghost. It was built by Sir Henry Griffith between 1598 and 1610. Anne Griffith, the youngest of his three daughters, was attacked by robbers on her way back from visiting friends. She died soon afterwards, at the hall, of her injuries. Her skull remains hidden somewhere in the house (at her request). If the skull is removed, it is said, her ghost will begin to walk, but as yet it remains safely bricked up in one of the old walls.

A headless horseman allegedly moves about the Quay at Bridlington.

At Skipsea, the wife of murderous knight Drogo de Bevere is said to haunt the area, periodically appearing as a lady wearing white. The apparition has been seen both during the night and in the day – sometimes with her head, and at other times without it. Eight hundred years is a long time for a ghost to wander…

In 1998 a haunting at a private house in Bessingby Road was reported in a local newspaper. The spirit was that of a Victorian gentleman, who had appeared ever since the family moved there a decade previously. The friendly ghost was witnessed both by the family and by visiting friends and neighbours. Phenomena included a mystery whirlwind that sent towels flying off the rails in the bathroom, a strong smell of tobacco appearing throughout the house and a ghostly voice which serenaded a startled visitor.

Bridlington Under Attack

1643: The Parliamentary Navy, at anchor in Bridlington Bay, bombarded the houses at the Quay where Queen Henrietta Maria sought refuge.

1779: Battle of Flamborough Head. A naval battle during the American War of Independence, this encounter was fought at sea between John Paul Jones in *Bonhomme Richard* and HMS *Serapis* of the Royal Navy.

First World War

1916: Enemy submarines sink HMS *Falmouth* in Bridlington Bay.

1917: A British airship flew over the town.

1918: Damage caused by an exploding mine close to the Beaconsfield sea wall.

1921: Cenotaph unveiled in Wellington Gardens, marked with the 331 names of the men lost in the First World War.

Second World War

During the Second World War many bombs fell on Bridlington. In 1940 bombs were dropped near the South Pier and properties damaged in Hilderthorpe Road and Springfield Avenue. The general post office on Quay Road was destroyed. Prospect Street, Manor Street and Prince Street were hit, including Foley's Café, the Woolworths store and the Cock & Lion. A mine explosion on South Foreshores damaged the golf club's house, and St George's Boys' School was bombed.

1941: In Lamplugh Road, St Anne's Convalescent Home and properties on the Promenade were hit.

The town adopted HMS *Bridlington*, a Bangor-class minesweeper. In 1941 the local WRVS sent a parcel of woollens to the sixty men on board and received their thanks. The vessel was not listed as an active unit in the 1945 Navy list; it was transferred to the RAF in 1946 and scrapped in 1958.

Local Dialect

Allus or Awlus – always

An'all – as well as/me too

Barmpot – fool

Blathered up – dirty

Blutherin – weeping noisily

Clarty – sticky

Click od – catch hold

Dab'and – expert, skilful

Dothery – unsteady

Ey-up – hello

Gawpin – staring

Hod on – wait

Jiggered – exhausted

Mafted – stifled, too hot

Mardy – moody, sulky

Maungy (Morn-jee) – sulky, spoilt, peevish

Mi-sen – myself

Nither – cold

Owt – anything

Rahve – pull, tear

Rollack – reprimand

Skeg – take a look at

Skelp – hit, beat

Snicket – alleyway between houses

Ta'en tiv – liked, accepted

Tha's nowt sa queer as folk – people can be odd/strange

Thisen – yourself

Thodd – third

Twonk – an idiot

Up-hod – uphold

Varry – very

Warnt – was not

Wesh – wash

Wi – with

Winnder – window

Yowp – shout

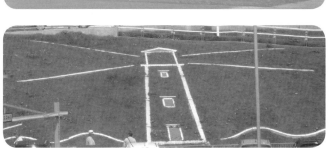

Festivals

European Open Beach Championship (fishing): £25,000 prize fund. Twenty years old, and held every March.

Beer Festival at the Prior John: March-April and also October.

Literature Festival, Scarborough, in April.

Bridlington Arts Festival in May.

Bridlington Golf Festival in May.

International Elvis Masters Championship (Elvis Weekender) in May.

Bridlington Festival of Running in May/June.

Bridlington Poetry Festival, Sewerby Hall, in June.

Old Town Summer Festival, in June/July.

Burton Agnes Jazz and Blues Festival, in July.

Summer Cider Festival, Prior John, in July.

Yorkshire Day, 1 August.

British Open Darts Championship, September/October.

Literature Festival, held in Beverley in October.

Sea Angling Festival, held in October since 1922.

Annual Vespa Scooter Rally in October.

Church Music Festival, in November.

Old Town Dickensian Festival, in December.

Filming Locations

The Royal: scenes filmed in Bridlington's High Street and elsewhere in the town.

The Brides in the Bath: Martin Kemp played the murderer George Joseph Smith in this ITV show, filmed in Old Town.

Antiques Road Trip featured the Georgian Rooms and the High Street. Charlie Ross and Charles James visited Bridlington Old Town.

Antiques Roadshow was filmed at the Spa in 1997 and 2008.

Ernest Whiteley & Co. (on the Promenade) featured in a documentary for local television.

Helicopter Heroes saved the day after an accident on the log flume at Bridlington seafront in 2011.

Sugar Town was filmed at John Bull Rock Factory (founded in 1911).

Scenes for *South Riding* were filmed here; Bridlington North Beach was Kiplington beach in the 2011 mini-series. Based on the novel *South Riding* by Winifred Holtby.

Rowan Tree Café was a location for *Supersize versus Superskinny* in 2012.

Rupert Grint (of *Harry Potter* fame) featured in a 2012 government-backed TV advert, carrying a surfboard on Bridlington beach to promote holidays in England and encourage Britons to holiday at home.

Recording of BBC Radio 4's *Just a Minute* took place at Bridlington Spa Theatre as part of the 2012 Arts Festival.

Legends of the Small and Silver Screen

The parents of Jenny Agutter, the film and television actress of *Railway Children* and *Midwives* fame, live in Bridlington.

Malcolm McDowell, the English actor, lived in Bridlington. Born Malcolm John Taylor in Leeds, his family relocated to the town. Known for his early roles in films *If....* (1968), *A Clockwork Orange* (1971), *O Lucky Man!* (1973), on which he is also credited as a writer, and *Caligula* (1979). Made his Hollywood debut as H.G. Wells in *Time After Time* (1979). Malcolm is known for many and varied roles in films and television series of different genres, but he has also appeared in several computer games. He currently resides in California.

Bridlington-born Peter Simon is a television presenter. He began his career at twelve years old on *Junior Showtime*, and was the first actor to play Ronald McDonald in a TV ad. Peter specialised in children's television at the beginning of his career, appearing on *Double Dare* and 'Run the Risk' on *Going Live*. He is currently an auctioneer on Bid Tv.

Shane Zaza, actor, attended Headlands School, Bridlington. Shane appeared in a small part in the film *The DaVinci Code* with Tom Hanks. On television he has appeared in *Mouth to Mouth*; *The Bill*; *Casualty*; *Dalziel & Pascoe*; *Doctors*; *Messiah*; *Murphy's Law*; *Spooks*; *The Omid Djalili Show*; and *Waterloo Road*.

Mark Herman (born in Bridlington) is an English film director and screenwriter. He directed and adapted *The Boy in the Striped Pyjamas* (2008). His first feature-length project was *Blame It on the Bellboy* (1992), he followed that by writing and directing the critically acclaimed *Brassed Off* (1996), about a struggling colliery brass band. Another of his well-known films is *Little Voice* (1998), adapted by Herman from Jim Cartwright's play *The Rise and Fall of Little Voice*. *Purely Belter* (2000) was adapted by Herman from Jonathan Tulloch's novel *The Season Ticket*. *Hope Springs* (2003), with Colin Firth and Minnie Driver, was also an adaptation – of *New Cardiff* by Charles Webb.

Artists

David Hockney, OM, CH, RA, was born in 1937 in Bradford. Today, he lives in Bridlington. Hockney is an internationally renowned and extremely influential English painter, draughtsman, printmaker, stage designer and photographer. He is a staunch pro-tobacco campaigner. A member of the Pop Art movement of the 1960s, his works include a series of paintings of swimming pools, the BMW 'art car' and 'A Bigger Grand Canyon', while 'Bigger Trees Near Warter', which measures 15 x 40ft, is a scale view of Woldgate coppice painted on fifty individual canvases. Hockney has also produced hundreds of portraits, still-lifes and landscapes using the iPhone and iPad.

His brother, Paul Hockney, has always been an artist, as well as a chartered accountant, recently specialising in iPhone art. Previously lived in Flamborough, but now in Bradford. His sister, Margaret Hockney, lives in Bridlington, and is a proponent of flatbed scanner art.

Michael Whitehand (born in Bridlington in 1941) is a self-taught artist. He has been painting since 1968, and is known for painting historical events and ships. He now lives in Cornwall.

Bands

Crescendo, formed in 2003, is an electronic pop duo. Liverpool-based, they comprise of Jonson Walker, from Bridlington, and Dan Ackerman.

International Rescue: a local band formed in 1980, and the band to hear in 1984, they reformed in 2011. The band comprises of Steve Skinner, Dave Waller, Chaz Cook and Joel Cash.

Sex Pistols Experience tribute act comprising Johnny Rotter, Kid Vicious, Steve Clones, and Paul Crook. John Lydon wished them good luck with it. The band originated in Bridlington in 2001. Dave Twigg (a.k.a. Paul Crook) is the only original member left.

The Sonnet: a local band, formed in 1996, comprising of Bridlington's Nick Tudor, with Will Clarke and Jason Lowe. Released the single 'Perfect Sunday'.

Edge of 13: a local band formed in 2010, they played at Liverpool's legendary Cavern Club in 2011. The band comprises of Kris MacLeod, Nick Asquith and Josie Fletcher.

Asio's Eyes: this band includes two local lads, Sam Howarth and Joel Whittaker. The other members are Tom Gabbatiss and Callum Topham. Their 'Atom Live' tour travelled around the UK in October 2012.

Musicians

Jonson Walker (see p98) is an English DJ and musician. He has released three self-financed EPs and released the EP 'Don't Let Them Tell You What To Do' on I Blame The Parents Records in early 2009. He has been based in Liverpool since 2000.

Ben Parcell was born, and still resides, in Bridlington. He is an English singer-songwriter and multi-instrumentalist. Since going solo in 2010 he has played over 130 shows around the UK supporting several established acts, and appearing on BBC. He was the lead singer and guitarist of pop punk band 'The Trailers' from 2002-2005. He creates music which he describes as pop folk.

Rolan Bolan's Band of 2006 can be seen in the image opposite. Rolan – the son of Marc Bolan of T Rex fame – is seated centre front. Vince 'Vinnyrock' Hall (of Bridlington) is standing at the back (right); Dave Lawry (of Bridlington) is seated on the left. The band's drummer, Bridlington's Jonny Blackmore, is seated on the far right.

Royalty

1319: Edward II spent a night in the prior's lodgings.

1415: Henry V gave thanks at St John's shrine after the battle of Agincourt.

1643: Queen Henrietta Maria landed in Bridlington with troops on the way back to York with armaments to support the Royalist cause in the English Civil War.

1785: Prince William Henry (William IV) landed in Bridlington.

1888: Prince Albert Victor opened Prince's Parade.

1928: Princess Mary opened Princess Mary Promenade.

1944: Visit of the king and queen with HRH Princess Elizabeth (on her first official engagement).

1976: Princess Margaret opened Station Avenue Health Centre.

1987: HRH The Duchess of Kent opened Leisure World.

1995: HRH The Duke of Gloucester opened the Promenades Shopping Centre.

1999: Prince Charles opened the MacMillan Cancer Ward at Bridlington Hospital.

Local Sportspeople

John Bintcliffe, Bridlington-born motor racer, won the Renault Clio Cup in 1994 and the Ford Credit Fiesta series in 1995. He is involved in the British Touring Car Championship as a driver for Audi, and is the team manager for the Bintcliffe Sport team.

Adam Khan was also born in Bridlington. He is a British sportsman and racing driver of Pakistani descent. Fluent in six languages, he has been part of the Formula Renault V6 Eurocup, the British F3 series and the A1 Grand Prix at Brands Hatch. Adam has competed in the six-race British Formula Ford series, the World Series by Renault, GP2 Asia Series, A1GP, and the Euroseries 3000; he joined the Renault F1 team in 2009. He was officially appointed as the ambassador for motor sports in Pakistan by the government.

David Pinkney is another Bridlington auto-racing driver. A semi-regular BTCC driver (1980s and 1990s), he briefly raced in the series in 2001, and has won the Vectra championship twice. His championship races include the Porsche Carrera Cup, the Seat Cupra Championship and the British Touring Car Championship (BTCC). He was injured in an eleven-car pile-up at Brands Hatch in 2007. After competing in the British GT Championship in 2008, he returned to the BTCC in 2009, driving for Team Dynamics. In 2010 Pinkney drove a Vauxhall Vectra run by his own team, Pinkney Motorsport. He opened the season with his first ever triple top-ten finish.

Mark Proctor, also of Bridlington, a British former Brands Hatch racing driver. Mark competed in the British Rallycross Championship and Eurocar BV8 series; the ASCAR series (stock-car racing); the British Touring Car Championship; and the Ginetta G50 Cup.

Bridlington martial arts instructor **Stuart Hicken** was made 10th Dan Grand Master and British representative to the World Martial Arts Association, Republic of China, in 2012. Prince Dschero Khan, the last living descendant of Mongolian warrior Ghengis Khan, bestowed the honour. The World Gathering of the Masters will be held in Bridlington in 2013.

Rugby

Facts about Bridlington Rugby Union Football Club:

Formed in 1924 from Bridlington School old boys, the club flourished. In the 1950s it moved to Dukes Park, their current home. In 1972 they got a new clubhouse.

Rugby players who went on to play county or senior rugby include John Lancaster (from 1950s); ten years later, Taff Harris, Alan Walker, John (Pansy) Potter, Orlando Lord, Mike Carvill and Doug Girking started playing (from the 1960s onwards).

Other players include Alex Scotter, who won many Yorkshire caps, and Ian Orum, part of England's touring side. Orum went professional with Castleford Rugby League. Steve Smith, who later became England captain, also played for them.

Local man Albert Thundercliffe propped for Yorkshire, and went on to Roundhay and Headingly.

A new wave of success started in 1986/87 with a record twenty-eight wins in a season.

Their first major trophy, 1987/88, was the Yorkshire Silver Trophy.

In 1988/89 they won the Yorkshire Shield.

The side were also League Champions two years running, winning Yorkshire Division 2.

The following years were very successful: Bridlington was promoted year on year through the Yorkshire and North East Divisions.

During this time a number of players gained county and England honours: Mike Cawthorne and Paul Evans, Karl Craggs, Neil Arton, Jonty Tilsley and John Clappison were playing for Yorkshire.

Recent years have seen success too: in 2012 they won the Yorkshire Shield.

Football

Semi-professional Bridlington Town AFC Football Club is based in Bridlington.

Nickname:
Seasiders.

Founded:
They were founded in 1918 as Bridlington Central United (re-formed in 1994).

Ground:
Queensgate has a capacity of 3,000 (740 seated).

Club Chairman:
Peter Smurthwaite.

Currently playing:
In the Northern Counties East Football League, Premier Division.

Major Honours:
FA Vase winner in 1993

FA Vase runners-up in 1990

ERCFA Senior Cup winners in 1921, 1922, 1923, 1931, 1953, 1957, 1961, 1965, 1967, 1970, 1972, 1989, 1993, 2005

NCEL Wilkinson Sword Trophy winners in 2002

NCEL Premier Division Champion winners in 2003 and 2010

More Local Sportspeople

Geoffrey Robinson is a local English cricketer, a left-handed batsman who fielded as a wicket-keeper, and could bowl slow left-arm orthodox (a particularly tricky type of spin). He is the son of Geoffrey Robinson Senior. Following in his father's footsteps, Geoffrey made his debut for Lincolnshire in 1965, and played minor counties cricket for Lincolnshire from 1965 to 1986.

Anthony David Towse is from Bridlington too. An English former first-class cricketer, he played one first-class match for Yorkshire County Cricket Club in 1988, appeared in one-day cricket for Lincolnshire in one game, and in eleven matches for the Wales Minor Counties.

International gymnast **Rebecca Owen** is from Bridlington. At the Commonwealth Games, in 2002, she won two silver medals in Manchester.

Craig Jonathan Short is a former football player from the town. A central-defender, his clubs include Blackburn Rovers, Derby County, Everton, Notts County, and Sheffield United. He was also manager of Notts County.

Richard Paul Wesley Cresswell is another Bridlington-born footballer. He was a striker for Sheffield United. Former clubs include Leeds United, Leicester City, Mansfield Town, Preston, Sheffield Wednesday, Stoke City, and York City.

Organised by Bridlington Road Runners, the 2011 October Half Marathon and fun run, assisted by the Rotary Club of Bridlington, proved very popular. The event was first held in 1983, originally by the local football team.

Heroes

Thomas Hopper Alderson GC (1903-1965) was the first civilian to be awarded the George Cross. An Air Raid Precautions Warden in Bridlington, he led teams into dangerous buildings to rescue trapped civilians during the Second World War.

Squadron Leader James Harry 'Ginger' Lacey DFM (1917-1989) died in Bridlington. He was one of the top-scoring Royal Air Force fighter pilots in the Second World War, and has a plaque at Priory church. He was also a flying instructor at Grindale aerodrome.

Gordon Harry Lakes MC (1928-2006) was born in Bridlington. Awarded the Military Cross in 1951, he was also former deputy director general in the UK Prison Service. A prison reformer, he is credited with helping to achieve improved working conditions among UK prisons. He saw action in the Korean War. Granted a CBE in 1987.

Leopold Dickson Romyn DSC (1902-1975) earned his medal in a dramatic way: in 1939, he waded into the sea and towed an enemy mine clear of Bridlington sea wall (having served in mine sweepers during the war).

Captain George Symons (1826-1871) VC, DCM. This hero died at Bridlington after a long life of service, which included action during the Crimean War, where he unmasked a five-gun battery. A commemorative plaque in The Priory has remembered him since 1989.

Lifeboat Heroes
Kit Brown (1842-1898) was a Bridlington fisherman and lifeboatman. In 1893 he rescued the crew of the sinking *Victoria*. Tragically, Brown was drowned in 1898 during a lifeboat disaster whilst rescuing a ship in distress. Two lifeboats were smashed under the sea wall during the attempted rescue.

Henry Freeman (1835-1904) was born in Bridlington. He later moved to Whitby, where he was a fisherman and lifeboatman for more than forty years.

Then & Now

Then & Now

Future Plans

Bridlington Regeneration Strategy

The Area Action Plan (AAP) is a ten-year programme (to 2021) to transform Bridlington with upwards of £170 million of public and private investment and the creation of 1,900 new jobs. The Spa project formed an important aspect of this strategy, which also includes a new shopping district, Burlington Parade, spaced between the coach park and Bridge Street, as well as 600 new houses in the area.

Bridlington Harbour Development

New harbour and a 320-berth marina and housing is planned, for mixed leisure and operational uses.

Sea Wall Defence Scheme

Protection work is planned (to 2014) to strengthen the most at-risk area, i.e the place where the wall joins the harbour's North Pier Corner to North Pier Junction and to Royal Prince's Parade, a 100-metre stretch of 140-year-old sea wall.

New Waterworks

Yorkshire Water Seafront Waterworks is to meet new European Union beach and sea-water standards by 2015. Improvements to the sewage system started in 2012; completion is set for April 2014, with a total estimated cost of £40 million. The improvements will comprise a new pumping station on Princess Mary Promenade, a large new sewer, and improvements to the existing sewer system (including work on the current pumping station). Finally, a new sea outfall, likely to cost up to £16 million, will be added to take storm water 2km out to sea. The vision is to see Yorkshire beaches and bathing waters become the best in Europe.

Fishing

Holderness Coast has been awarded £1.15 million from the European Fisheries Fund and DEFRA to help the local fishing industry and fishing communities between Flamborough and Spurn point. The money is to be spent between December 2011 and 2015.

Homelessness to be addressed

Bridlington is a recognised hot spot for rough sleepers and homelessness. In October 2011, East Riding Yorkshire Council were offered £308,000 in government funding from the Homes and Communities Agency to provide short-term accommodation for nine people at a time, all manned for 24 hours. The money is also to provide healthcare, probation, training and employment. Subject to contract; it will be completed by autumn of 2013.

National Grid

By 2015 the National Grid, an underground pipeline, will be in place to carry carbon-dioxide waste from a West Yorkshire power station, via a preferred route of Barmston, to storage caverns beneath the North Sea seabed.

East Riding of Yorkshire Council Waste Management

Plans include the cutting of landfill, and the achieving of a recycling and composting target of 60-65 per cent by 2020.

Leisure World (opened 1987) to be Re-Vamped!

The plan involves a total demolition and rebuild estimated at £17 million. The facility is to close in September 2013, and re-open in April 2015.

Sewerby Hall Restoration Project

£2.6 million will be spent on this: £1 million from the Heritage Lottery Fund, with East Riding Yorkshire Council to contribute another £1.6 million. This is a phased project, due to run from autumn of 2012 to summer of 2014.

Things to Do

Stroll along Bridlington's south-side Promenade and enjoy the nautical mile. (The mile officially opened in 1999.) ☐

Take a dip in the sea then use the open-air showers to wash away salty water and sand. ☐

Visit Bridlington Spa exhibitions and return in the evening for one of the spectacular shows. ☐

Eat fish and chips on the harbour whilst watching commercial fishermen and call in at the Harbour Heritage Museum. ☐

Follow the Bridlington Maritime Trail. ☐

Take a trip out to sea; choices include fishing, speedboat, pirate ship and the RSPB Gannet and Puffin Cruise on the *Yorkshire Belle* to view the seabird colony at Bempton. ☐

Walk along north-side Promenade taking in the natural beauty of the cliffs. ☐

Hire a deckchair or chalet, and take a swim – with lifeguards on duty during the summer. ☐

Ride the land train to Sewerby Park, Hall and Zoo; then explore Sewerby village and the Bondville Miniature Model Village. ☐

Meander up the quaint historic Old Town, browse the High Street antique shops and art galleries, and enjoy the lovely Georgian buildings. Follow the Old Town Trail. ☐

Visit Bridlington's Priory church, celebrating 900 years since its founding as an Augustinian priory in 1113. ☐

Visit the Bayle Museum. ☐

Websites

www.aboutbridlington.co.uk

www.asios-eyes.com

www.ba-education.com

www.bridlington.co.uk

www.dataobs.eastriding.gov.uk

www.forgework-bridlington.co.uk (David Cooper blacksmith)

www.bridlingtonfreepress.co.uk

www.bridlingtongolfclub.co.uk

www.bridlington.gov.uk (Town Council)

www.bridlingtonlifeboat.co.uk

www.bridlingtonmartialarts.com

www.bridlington.net

www.bridlingtonrfc.co.uk (Rugby Club)

www.bridlingtonrr.co.uk (Road Runners)

www2.Bridlingtontoday.co.uk/history/timeline.asp

www.bridsailingcoble.org.uk (*Three brothers* cobble)

www.eastriding.gov.uk (East Riding Yorkshire Council)

www.edgeof13.co.uk

www.freespiritwriters.me.uk (Mike Wilson)

www.genuki.org.uk

www.ons.gov.uk

www.rolanbolan.co.uk

www.sexpistolsexperience.co.uk

www.ukskydivingadventures.com/Bridlington

www.vespa.org.uk

www.yorkshire.com/places/yorkshire-coast/bridlington

Picture Credits

Unless otherwise credited, pictures are from the author's collection.

Page:

Bibliography

Bridlington Free Press Newspaper

Bridlington Library Local Studies

Neave, David & Susan (2000), *Bridlington: An introduction to its History & Buildings*

Neave, David (2000), *Port Resort and Market Town: A History of Bridlington*

Pugh, R.B. (Ed.) (1974), *The Victoria History of the County of York East Riding Vol. II*

Stockton, N. (Ed.) (1999), *East Riding Dialect Dictionary 2nd ed.* (East Riding Dialect Society)

Whitworth, Alan (2001), *Foul Deeds and Suspicious Deaths on the Yorkshire Coast*

Wilson, Mike (2008), *My Bridlington Old and New*

Wilson, Mike (2009), *More Bridlington Then and Now*